From Piece to Peace

From Piece to Peace

By: Je'Nae Brown

"From Piece to Peace"

Published by: New Voice Books LLC
Contact number: 972-637-3321
Website: nvpublishingco.com
Cover design by Halo Creative Services
ISBN: 979-8-9898714-2-1
Library of Congress Number:

Printed in the United States of America

Table of Contents

Preface

Welcome to From Piece to Peace

Tit for tat. That's what my mom used to say when she did something for someone, but wanted something in return. I've always done things for people, intending not to receive anything back, but then there's this void or feeling of loneliness and regret. Most of the time, the people I am giving to never ask for it. They might hint, but it's never blunt. My heart is so big that if I sense that someone is in need, or just having a hard time with something, I try to offer or do whatever I can.

I have to save them. These Clark Kent tendencies are starting to affect me. I'm recognizing that people don't show up for me like I show up for them. There is nothing mutual going on in my life at this present time. I never voice that I'm in need and that I want them to commit to me like I commit to them. As I look back and trace my steps to see where I went wrong, I can't seem to find the answer. I reference this trait that I have to a pocket. You can use pockets to put things in and remove things when you want to, but the pocket never has a say so, as to what it can retain.

The pocket can get so heavy at times, but it holds on and cherishes the things that fill it up and never complains. It remains humble and patient, waiting to be exploited, and when it's empty, its loneliness overtakes what once was stability. The pocket is weak without stability. So, at this very moment, I feel weak, used, and lifeless. I feel that I have no use in this world because no one is using me. I want people to feel what I feel, but instead, I just remain calm, cool, and collected until another user comes along, then I'm alive again, happy and free. Being mutual is the tit-for-tat that I yearn for.

In sharing this experience, I hope to reach those who feel like they're constantly giving without receiving. This reflection will help you recognize when relationships are imbalanced and how to set healthy boundaries. You'll learn how to express your needs, create mutual support, and avoid the emptiness that comes from one-sided giving. By the end of this book, you may find the strength to reclaim your energy and transform your relationships into something more balanced and fulfilling. I want you to understand the importance of harmony, self-awareness, and emotional barriers.

Introduction

I used to believe that peace was something you found outside of yourself, buried in the arms of another, hidden in the approval of those you love, or waiting just beyond the next accomplishment. I chased it relentlessly, thinking if I just did more, gave more, endured more, I'd finally feel whole. But every time I thought I had it, life reminded me that I was still searching. Searching is an intention and should result in whatever you're looking for being found. But when you have no idea of what you're searching for, how can that result be retrieved?

So, I woke up every day, intentionally searching, hoping, believing that I would find my peace. I have been broken more times than I can count. Shattered by love, by loss, by my reflection staring back at me, asking why I wasn't enough. And for a long time, I let the broken pieces of me define the whole. I lived in survival mode, mistaking it for strength. But peace, real peace, doesn't come from running, proving, or waiting for someone else to hand it to you. It comes from within.

This book is a journey, not of finding peace, but of becoming it. Of taking every piece of yourself that was once shattered and learning how to place them not back where they were, but where they were always meant to be. Throughout your reading of this book, I want you to set everything aside. Set aside your problems, worries, burdens, future, past, even the good, and I want you to take those pieces and make them whole. I want you to find you. If you've ever felt like life has broken you beyond repair, I hope these pages remind you that nothing is beyond restoration and even you are worthy of fixing you.

Chapter 1

Nothing

I wanted to be the first person that you could count on without being asked to be counted. To give is ***to freely transfer the possession of something to someone***, and every time I gave, I felt a sense of freedom. Yet, with each act of giving, my loneliness grew. It's like being in a classroom where the teacher asks a question, and I'm the first to raise my hand, not because I know the answer, but because I want to be the first who's called upon. That's what giving has been to me. A way to be the first person you can rely on, even without you asking. I would give my life to save someone who has ever been in need.

Ever since I was a child, I've had this innate ability to see the need in people. While everyone has five senses, I've always had six. When you look up empathy in the dictionary, you might see my picture beside it. This extra sense allows me to see the need in people, whether it's a shoulder to lean on or a helping hand, I was there. I've never thought of myself as superior or divine; I just have this strong feeling when someone is in need. So, I give.

I must say that my life was pretty enjoyable growing up. We always had a roof over our heads, food on the table, and clothes on our backs. I was privileged to have had both my parents in one household, so there were no complaints. They raised three beautiful children, and those years were some of the best years of my life. I wouldn't change a thing if I could go back. God's presence was heavy throughout my childhood. My dad was a preacher, and my great-grandmother was the mother of the church, so I had no choice but to go to church often.

The relationship that I had with God wasn't always what it needed to be, but what should your relationship with God be like as a child? Every experience, whether a moment of joy or a challenge, has shaped me into who I am today. The traits and even the bad habits I picked up along the way have played their part in my growth. I've learned that every lesson is truly a blessing, no matter if it comes from success or hardship. You have to walk through these lessons to discover your best self, and I'm grateful for the path that has led me here.

In middle school, I always enjoyed physical education. It was a time when we were free for about 45 minutes. Although sometimes the gym teacher would have an activity for us to do, it was still a refreshing part of the day. I remember one day we were learning the fundamentals of a certain sport. We were each taking turns, and it was time for one of my friends to give it a try. When she gave it her all, she didn't master the task. So, the gym teacher we had at the time yelled at her for failing.

My empathy senses went off and I yelled, "Give her a chance!". The gym teacher didn't like it one bit, cursed at me for saying something, and then told me to leave the gym. I walked out with tears in my eyes. All I could think of was, how could someone be so cruel when all I was doing was being there for a friend? I should have been praised for taking up for her, not cursed at. I felt that I didn't have a voice. I promised myself that from then on, I would be there for anyone who needed me, and that no one would interfere with my willingness to help.

As I grew older, I discovered that my sixth sense was now focused on the men who came in and out of my life. Here I am, a single mother with two of the most handsome boys that I birthed, but still catering to men who probably never even cared that I existed. How am I supposed to teach my two kings how not to take advantage of a giving woman, when all their mother did was give to men who weren't worthy of her time? I felt that the only way to love was to give. So, I always did everything in my power to make sure those I was with at the time felt that love.

The more I gave, the more they took. I'm not in any way, shape, or form bashing them, I'm just speaking my truth. I had given so much of myself that I had lost myself. I had lost the woman that I was becoming because I wanted to give all of her to someone else. I know now that isn't possible without reciprocation. You cannot give your all to someone who does not match your energy and expect everlasting happiness. That person will take from you until you're completely unrecognizable. Losing oneself can happen gradually and often goes unnoticed until the person feels completely disconnected from their true self.

Below are some common ways this can occur:

1. Neglecting Self-Care: Constantly putting others' needs above your own can lead to burnout and a loss of identity.

2. Living for Others: Making decisions based on what others want or expect from you, rather than what you truly desire, can cause you to lose touch with your aspirations and values.

3. Suppressing Emotions: Ignoring or bottling up your feelings can create a disconnect between your actions and your true emotions.

4. Lack of Boundaries: Allowing others to overstep your personal boundaries can lead to a feeling of being overwhelmed and controlled.

5. Chronic Stress and Anxiety: Ongoing stress and anxiety can cloud your mind and make it difficult to recognize your own needs and desires.

6. Ignoring Personal Passions: Abandoning hobbies and interests that once brought you joy can make life feel monotonous and unfulfilling.

7. Unhealthy Relationships: Being in relationships where you are not valued or respected can erode your self-esteem and sense of self.

8. Constant Change and Instability: Frequent changes in life circumstances without taking time to adapt and reflect can make it hard to maintain a stable sense of identity. Reconnecting with yourself often involves self-reflection, setting healthy boundaries, and prioritizing activities and relationships that align with your true self.

Every day when I looked in the mirror, I didn't know who was looking back at me. People should look in the mirror and immediately love the person that they see. I saw nothing. It got so bad that my presence was dull. There was a lack of stimulation, and I had isolated myself from the world. My dad would often call me on the phone and would tell me that something about me had changed. He would tell me that I didn't sound like myself, or that he could see the hurt. All I saw was nothing.

So, I didn't understand what others were witnessing, because I didn't see it for myself. I would go to work and cry while sitting at my desk. Then, when I got home, I would go to my room, lie down, and not come out until the next morning. There were no interactions with my two boys, and I knew they could see the pain that was taking over me. I saw nothing. This defeat was draining every part of me to the point that the only thing I was praying for was death. I often joked with my mom that when I passed away, I wanted her to send out invitations to my funeral because everyone couldn't come. I would call her and say, "Get those invites ready," and we would laugh about it, but deep down, I was so sincere.

The nothing that I was seeing had now become my identity. I became a shadow of who I once was, lost in a void where my identity used to be. I didn't want people to see the nothing that I had become. I was stagnant, and every breath that I let out during that period was cold. Life felt like it was passing me by while I remained frozen in place, unable to move forward or feel the warmth of genuine connection and joy. How could I let myself go to waste and not have the confidence to move? I had become paralyzed by my doubts and insecurities, watching as life unfolded around me without being able to take a step toward reclaiming my path.

For every connection that I freely gave to, a void was birthed. Birthing something is supposed to be beautiful, but these voids felt like torture. Like an undoing of something that once was. It was a discomfort that I couldn't fathom. Initially, I thought that the start of every encounter would fill the voids that had been produced. They were like placeholders, temporary gaps waiting to be filled by the next connection. I recognized they weren't merely spaces; they were wounds, unseen yet undeniably felt. Instead, my unwanted mishaps had transformed into avoidances. I acknowledged that the voids were there, but I chose to ignore them. I couldn't stare too long into the emptiness. Avoiding a void was the easiest thing I could do for my sanity.

I often wondered what if. What if I could avoid what needed to be done and feel accomplished? What would I see if I did? Myself, my failures, my unmet needs? Avoidance was my safety, and there was absolutely no other way. Avoidance brought me temporary relief, but it wasn't healing. If anything, it kept me locked in a cycle. An endless loop of hoping someone or something else could do the work I was unwilling to do for myself. It wasn't until I began to sit with the voids, naming them, feeling them, that I realized their power didn't come from what they were missing, but from what they were asking of me. To face them was to face me. I didn't want to choose reality, so avoidance had become my best friend.

At the beginning of this book, I referred to the nothing identity I took on to a pocket. I had gotten so heavy, but I never said a word. I had felt that if I said anything or acted impatient, I would lose my stability. This sixth sense that I had carried for so many years turned me into this weak, used, lifeless nothing. Who was going to save me? Who was going to build me back into something? I realized that the only one who could save me was me. It dawned on me that waiting for others to lift my spirits was futile. The power to change my life and reclaim my strength was within me, and the inner struggles and challenges that I was facing had to cease. My generous, unbalanced, and unappreciated heart could no longer give without reciprocity.

Below you'll find a list of ways and examples of how you can overcome seeing nothing:

1. **Communicate Your Needs**: It's important to let others know when you need support. Expressing your needs doesn't make you less generous; it makes your relationships more balanced and authentic.

Example: "I've been there for you in tough times, and right now, I could use some support myself."

2. **Set Boundaries**: Ensure you are not overextending yourself. Setting boundaries can help you manage your energy and prevent feelings of being used.

Example: "I want to help, but I also need time for myself. How about we find another solution?"

3. **Evaluate Relationships**: Take a step back and assess which relationships are reciprocal and which are one-sided. Focus more on the relationships that offer mutual support.

Example: "I've noticed that our interactions are often about your needs. Can we talk about how to make our relationship more balanced?"

4. Self-Care and Self-Worth: Engage in activities that make you feel valued and happy outside of helping others. Building your self-worth independently can reduce the feeling of emptiness.

Example: "I'm going to dedicate some time each week to activities I enjoy and that fulfill me personally."

5. Seek Mutual Connections: Surround yourself with people who naturally give as much as they take. This can create a more fulfilling social environment.

Example: "I'm looking to build connections with people who value reciprocal support and kindness."

Do you remember when you rode your bike without training wheels for the first time or received your driver's license and felt that it was you against the world? It's a rush of excitement, and you feel that no one can get in your way or stop you from becoming this new human being that you have become. I might be exaggerating, but I'm sure you get where I'm going with this. People should never be able to take any kind of joy away from you. Who are they to tell you how to feel? **Ephesians 4:32 NIV** says, ***"Be kind and compassionate to one another, forgiving each other, just as Christ God forgave you"***. Now I know I don't go by everything that the Bible says like I'm supposed to, and I'm far from perfect. I do know that being kind, compassionate, and forgiving should be a way of life.

I do question sometimes why Jesus endured everything that he went through. There was so much pain, yet he was stable through it all. People often show fear when there are things that they cannot change. I wonder if it's something that is out of their control, or is it just a feeling of defeat? If it is defeat, then that feeling can take over and make you not want to fight for what it is that you want. Ok, you lost one, two, three, four times, so you bury it nine feet under and never look back. Why should you keep trying if nothing is working? Can several failed attempts be a loss? I can't answer that question for you, but I can encourage you to never lose hope.

Chapter 2

Hope

As I hang on to the edge of this precipice, a stark cliff overlooking the turbulent sea below, I start to reminisce on all the things I've done, said, could've said, and even could've been. Was it really that bad? Hanging on to this edge has opened my eyes to a new reality, but is it too late? Should I try to save myself, or should I just fall and let the ground take my hope? What am I even hanging on for? There is no reassurance, stability, or growth. It's just a cycle that I keep reliving.

My fingers keep slipping, and I can hear the sweat rolling off my forehead hitting the ground far below. "Hang on…fight…be strong," races through my mind. Maybe someone will grab my hand, pull me up, and tell me that everything is going to be okay. But I've been hanging on this edge for a while. No one is coming, so I think it's time to let go. In that moment of decision, I realized that letting go doesn't mean giving up, it means finding a new path, a new way to hope. I take a deep breath, loosen my grip, and embrace the fall, ready to discover what lies beyond the edge.

In the past, I had always felt that the fight was over. I have endeavored so much, and most of the time I've failed. Trying something that you've attempted to accomplish over and over again can be so tiring that it seems easier to eradicate it from your mind forever. Failing often altered my ability to see the good in me. It put me in a dark space in my life. I felt that no one was on my side, and I needed someone to agree with me. I've learned to never look for validation in others and not to wait for anyone to be my hope.

The very first moment that I realized my hope had diminished was when all of the silent screaming and invisible tears were no longer affecting me. I also realized that even the most intense internal pain stops making a difference. Those moments made me wonder, was it relief, or was it just the realization that I'd lost something essential? Essential things are important. So, I knew that my evaporated hope needed to find its place again, but I was just blind to who had taken it. The pain never shook me. It never demanded to be felt. It was just there, playing over and over again as if my life were a broken record. I wanted to mend myself back together. I wanted to fix the pieces that once made me whole. Instead, I chose to continuously wipe the invisible tears that had fallen and just counted them as another loss.

I used to repeat these affirmations every morning, *"Is it really that bad? How can I change the course of my life with a different choice"?* I never really had the answers to those questions, but it did make me feel good saying them. Feeling good about myself was the first step. I knew that I had to have hope to redirect my life. I would listen to motivational YouTube videos, play music that was soothing to my soul, and most of the time sit on my bed and write. To me, writing was my getaway from the world, but that's all that I did. I never progressed past the first step.

There were no actions. Then one day, I just started writing down all of the things that I was hopeful for. I had the intention that if I saw it on paper, then maybe hope would appear. There was so much that I was going through at that time, but I had to persevere. I had to show my two African American Kings that their mom was able to conquer anything. As all of this was transpiring, I was also finishing up my third year of graduate school. Yes, I said third year, and yes, I do know that most graduate programs should be completed within two years.

I was enduring so much at that time that focusing was not my priority. I had failed many classes, and it was because I didn't have the motivation to press forward. I didn't want to let go of what was, in order for me to gain what could have been. They say that the minimum amount of faith that you need is the size of a mustard seed. I looked for that seed for so long and never retrieved it. It had gotten so bad that my professors would reach out to me asking if there was anything that they could do to help. I didn't want their assistance, I just wanted to hang onto the edge of the cliff patiently. Every Good Samaritan that God sent my way to help me, I dismissed.

I kept telling myself that no one wanted to help me, but I yearned for someone to reach out at the same time. It's like I didn't want to grab anyone's hand to pull me over that edge. When you hang onto something that isn't for you for so long, it can become a part of you. It develops more and more every day, and you start to see less of the hope that you need. At first, you might question it, but after a while, it numbs you. You no longer have feelings. Your dreams begin to vanish, and you lose all sight of your future. Where is the hope? That numbness was so real. People would talk to me, and it would just go in one ear and out the other. I didn't want to hear what I should have done to prevent what I was going through, and I couldn't stand it when someone was right. This lack of hope had turned me into a stone. Still, yet waiting to be built.

During this time of hanging onto the edge, I thought I had found my person. It started amazingly, and it was something that I never thought I'd find. That amazing excitement that I had witnessed was so momentous that I blocked out the rest of my life. A life that I had known for years, but this one person had expunged it. He took away every breath that had left my body, instead of taking my breath away. Where was my hope? I remember the very first day he laid a hand on me, and no, it wasn't in an affectionate way. The hit was so painful that I couldn't shed one tear. Have you ever felt a pain so deep that tears wouldn't come? This pain was subtle.

It worsened every day, and every one of those days, I was so sure that it would get better. The better that I was praying for never showed up for me. He would disappear Friday through Sunday and tell me that he was going on these work trips. One morning, while he was away on one of those so-called trips, I awoke to an accidental voicemail that he'd left on my phone. The voicemail consisted of his and another woman's voice.

He was explaining to her why he couldn't talk to her during the week, and she was just taking it all in. That was the first time that I had experienced pillow talk through a voicemail. My heart had already been shattered, but this time the pieces just got stepped on. When I called him, of course, he denied every allegation. He didn't get home until later that night, and he just walked through the door as if nothing had happened. I didn't say a word. There was no hope.

He asked if I wanted to go out, and I agreed because I thought that if we went out, hope would appear. As I was in the bathroom doing my makeup, the woman who had taken my place called his phone. He wasn't around, so I answered. She started asking me questions like who I was and why I had his phone. As she awaited my response, I took a deep breath of what I had left and said, "You stole my heart." She started yelling at the top of her lungs, but I couldn't respond. The pain, full of no tears, had recurred. I couldn't even move. It's like I was stuck in a thought that couldn't be expressed.

Before I could hang up, he walked into the bathroom and noticed I had answered. As he snatched the phone and hung it up, the very hand that he had laid on me before had gone across my back. I fell to the floor from the impact, but still no tears, just pain. He had always used force instead of letting me explain my decisions. He then started to yell at me, asking why I had answered his phone, and that whoever was on the other line was none of my business. I had no words to exchange with him. I waited for him to leave the bathroom before I stood up and got myself together. I took all of my clothes and makeup off, lay in my bed, and barricaded myself underneath my comforter. All hope was lost.

If you haven't figured it out by now, his hand was the hope that I was looking for to pull me up from that edge. Which is why I refused any other hand. I wanted him to pull me up and tell me that I didn't need to worry anymore. I wanted him to apologize for everything that he had put me through. I wanted him to acknowledge the fact that I was his only love. I wanted him to need me as badly as I thought I needed him. I wanted him to feel the pain from his hands that he had released upon me. I wanted him to mend my heart.

There's this popular saying that you can't always get what you want. It took me almost three years to understand that wanting something can be satisfactory, but the need for that something can end up equivocal. I didn't need him to be my hope. All I needed was to prepare myself for what was on the ground from the fall and embrace every obstacle, opportunity, dream, and healing mindset that was in my path to finding my hope. I needed to live in the present.

Chapter 3

The Present

Nicole sat by the window, watching the rain trickle down the glass. She clutched a worn letter, its words now meaningless. For years, she had stayed with Jacob, clinging to the hope that he would become the man she imagined. She ignored the present, the nights he came home late, the coldness in his eyes, the emptiness in their conversations. She thought about their recent argument. She had wanted to scream, to tear him down with every bitter word lodged in her throat. But she didn't. Instead, she swallowed her pain, fed by the hope that he would change.

Their intimacy was no different. She lay beneath him, eyes closed, pretending it was everything she dreamed. But dreams were just that, fleeting, intangible. Nicole realized she had been living in a future that might never come, ignoring the present that screamed for her attention. She looked out at the rain, feeling each drop as a call to wake up. It was time to see Jacob for who he truly was, not who she wished him to be. With a deep breath, she let the letter fall from her fingers. It landed softly, like the last petal of a dying rose. The future could wait. It was time to embrace the present.

It all started with a dm on a dating site. I can't remember the exact words that were sent to me, but I do remember the fine, dark complexion of his skin. It looked so smooth; I touched my phone screen and rubbed the side of his face. All I could think was, he is too good to be true. I just knew that he was supposed to be a part of my path. I had to have him. As soon as we exchanged numbers, he called. That was the best four-hour conversation that I'd ever had. I forgot about the world during that phone call. It was just me and him. How could he make me feel this way? I am a Scorpio, so my emotions are always at a perpetual high. During that phone call, I discovered that he was a Scorpio as well. Our emotions coincided with one another, and we didn't want it to end.

It took him only two days to ask me to be his woman, and I gladly accepted. I did think about it before my acceptance, but after I thought, why is he asking me so soon, and am I stable enough to be in a relationship right now? These thoughts only lasted for about 30 seconds. I was willing to take the risk, and no one could stop me or change my mind. We often talked about our future, how we would get married, and just live life to the fullest. He had made so many promises to me that all I could look forward to was the future.

I was only about two months in with the person who had stolen my breath, leaving me empty rather than complete. There was never any uplifting in any way, instead, he consumed me, leaving me gasping for air. Our relationship was something that should have been so beautiful, but instead, it had turned into something that suffocated my spirit. I didn't notice at first how each sigh of frustration, each whispered apology, and each moment I held my tongue chipped away at the air I needed to survive. I gave pieces of myself without question, believing that love requires sacrifice. But somewhere in the giving, I forgot that love is also supposed to give back. I became breathless, not from passion, but from exhaustion. I was choking on silence, swallowing my voice just to keep the peace. Every breath I had once used to laugh, to dream, to speak life into myself had been stolen, leaving me hollow.

The thing about breath is that it's stubborn. Even when you feel like you can't catch it, it fights to return. I remember the moment I finally exhaled, not in surrender, but in release. I let go of the weight I had carried, the pain I had swallowed, and the silence that had suffocated me. With that breath came a whisper, faint but clear, telling me that I was still here. And with that whisper, I inhaled. Deeply. Fully. For myself, this time.

Before I could finally catch my breath, I was starting to see that most of his promises were just words. Unfortunately, I didn't have any idea of what red flags were and how to detect them until this relationship. I had done a little bit of research and found out that red flags were behaviors that could be violent, manipulative, controlling, and even jealous. A red flag could be any kind of problem or issue that you detect in someone that isn't in your best interest, or to your liking.

One of the first red flags that I became aware of was how he would text, call, and even FaceTime me during the day, but at night, there was silence from him. At the end of his day, he would talk on the phone with me all the way home and even sit in the car for a while, but when it was time to go into the house, I didn't hear from him again until the next morning. This red flag is probably more common than most. I was working 12-hour shifts at the time, so I would fall asleep as soon as we hung up.

The next morning, I noticed that he had never called me back after we had hung up. I didn't let him know that I was going to sleep, nor did we say goodnight to each other. The phone calls always ended with I'll call you back. So, I just concluded that maybe he wanted me to get some rest since he knew that I had to be at work early the next morning. Assuming can easily take over your mind and blind you to seeing what's really there. There were so many red flags that I saw at the very beginning, but I chose to keep looking ahead. The future was definitely more exciting than the present.

My sixth sense was radiating even more in this relationship. All he did was take, and I'll admit that most of the time I offered, but there was never anything in return, and if there was, he would want immediate recognition for it. I would often think to myself how much dumber could I be, all while trying to figure out where my common sense had escaped. Once again, these were just thoughts that came and went. I thought that this was love, and I didn't want to lose it. I kept telling myself that if I had walked away, I would never find anyone else like him.

Not realizing that I didn't need him. I could just feel the future getting close. I could feel the breakthrough that we needed was just around the corner. While waiting and feeling for something that I could not see, pain had entered into my relationship. The pain was very feathery when it entered, but over time, it became a brick. I couldn't lift it even if I tried. We needed a shift, but the heaviness wouldn't let us move. I noticed that the only one who was trying to take a step forward was me.

It was always my longing for improvement. The future was near. There were a lot of good traits to him, and most of the time, he could be as sweet as me. I saw the enormous heart that he had, so I often lost sight and exchanged the bad for the good. I can't say that he wined and dined me; instead, I wined and dined him. I did look forward to the flowers that would be on the counter when I got home every now and then, but that was all that I received. It was something, so I was appreciative. When he looked at me, I would always see this sparkle in his eyes, but that sparkle had a sense of evil to it. Instead of questioning my inner thoughts, I persisted in looking forward. The future was two blocks away.

The evil spark presented itself more as time passed by. Sometimes I was too afraid to speak because I knew that if I had opened my mouth for anything, the results would not be to my liking. I had colored all the red flags green, but couldn't color within the lines. I always wanted to go everywhere that he went and didn't want to leave his side. Whether it was to the store, gas station, bar, or anywhere. There were times when I would often look out the window when I heard a car door slam, because I thought it was him coming back home to me.

Most of those times, it wasn't him. He wasn't the type who would call me to let me know where he was or just to provide any updates. So, I was always calling and texting as if I were this needy person who didn't have any other priorities. Now maybe I was already a little crazy before I met him, but his actions had made my addiction heighten. While he didn't have a care in the world to cure my addiction, I looked past it all, striving for the greatness ahead. The future was down the street. By this time, I couldn't see a thing. All of the good that I had wanted him to reveal was lost in space.

A space that I could never grab hold of. I had become a tree. I couldn't move or even find the strength to try. I was a tree full of branches, extending each one of them to him. He wasn't watering the tree that I had become, and I was beginning to dry up each day. I thought that he would be my roots and keep me whole and stable, but instead, he took every nutrient that I needed for growth. The vibrant green I once wore turned brittle and brown, and I could feel myself drying up with every passing moment.

Yet I kept reaching out to him, kept offering my shade, my fruit, my very essence, hoping he would notice the tree he was slowly diminishing. There was no future. It never made it to my front door, and it never presented itself like I had hoped it would. I had nothing to look forward to, and I just had to accept the present. Sometimes we only stay because of the hope and the potential that we want them to be, instead of seeing what they are in the present. It's easy to get lost in our hopes and desires, but recognizing and accepting the present is crucial for genuine fulfillment and growth.

Staying anchored in reality helps us make better choices and avoid the pitfalls of self-deception. We can feed off of our *"wants"* so much. Those *"wants"* give us the energy to deal with their bullshit every day. It bites our tongue when we want to tear down every piece of them with our words. It even blinds us when they're lying on top of us, thinking that they're giving us the best intercourse we've ever had. Those *"wants and hopes"* can be so deceiving that we never witness their true selves. So, we stay in those *"hopes and wants"* for days, months, and years, prayerful that the future will work in our favor. We ignore the present for an anticipated future, letting all time pass us by.

Chapter 4

Time

Does time really heal all wounds? After my last serious relationship, I felt so shattered that I wanted to bury my head in the sand and mourn until my last breath. Here I am, three years later, still feeling broken. What time were they referring to? I haven't healed, and every day, my mind is consumed by this pain. When someone or something possesses you, you're being controlled or owned. That's exactly how I felt in that relationship, and as the years have passed, I haven't evolved. Where is the healing?

It is now 10:31 pm; will this be the start time of this broken clock? From that time, I couldn't seem to find comfort in anything that I had succeeded in or tried to accomplish. Although I was no longer in that horrific relationship, there was still this void, and I didn't know how to put my finger on what it was. All I knew was that I needed to heal, but there was no inspiration to do so. So here I am again, looking for a hand from someone else. It was like washing your clothes.

You put your clothes inside the washer and add detergent, and any other liquid to your liking, depending on what you're washing, of course. Then, when you close the lid, the washer starts its cycle. Within this cycle, there are different stages. There is a washing stage, a resting stage, a rinse stage, and then a final spin stage. I always started the cycle, but when the final spin was complete, the results were still unclean. I knew that I had to throw myself into the washer, but I could never grasp the purpose of why I would throw myself in there. Awaiting that start time.

Healing should be an intimate and transformative personal journey. I feel that it's ok to take longer than you expected. No one should ever be able to tell you how to heal, when to heal, or why you should heal. It should come only from within you. You should be able to tell yourself that healing could be vital to embracing you again. Things can change for the better, but at the same time, that better can come and go. I used to believe that healing was just a mindset, but oftentimes my mind still wandered. I had to heal my soul in order not to take that last breath. Is the clock still broken?

Wash stage

In the wash stage, all my emotions and experiences were churned and agitated, much like the clothes in a washing machine. It was like there was still something holding me back. I was forced to confront everything that had been buried deep within, but I didn't want to. I do know that the urge to feel anything was very substantial during this stage. If I could just find love, then I would be content. Once again, I was back on my bullshit.

I was back giving and not receiving anything. I was falling for masked men who never once revealed their faces. I kept asking myself, what was it about me that was drawing in the fake and not the real? I wanted to feel the real so badly that I was still blind to all of the deceit. This didn't stop the painful memories from resurfacing; I knew I had to face them head-on. It wasn't easy; in fact, it was incredibly painful. But it was necessary. What time is it now?

Rest stage

During the rest stage, I allowed myself to pause and reflect. Although I didn't give myself much time to pause. I was often in and out of my thoughts, pondering on my next move. Initiating things was my forte. My favorite text to send was, "Would you like to go out for drinks later?". I felt that text would reel them in and hook them onto me. We might've gone out for drinks and had the best night, but after that, they would always escape the hook.

Then here comes my thoughts again, saying that wasn't successful, let's try this one more time. That one more never ended, it only matured. This was a critical part of my healing journey, yet there was still no healing. I did give myself permission to feel the pain, the sadness, and the loneliness. This is when I realized that my tears were no longer dry. After another failed attempt, I would dispose of all my pain onto my steering wheel.

My car was my resting place. It was the place where I sent the infamous text. It was the place where I did the short pausing and reflecting. It was the place where I would listen to songs like Cut It Out by Tink, Congratulations by Alicia Creti, My Mind by Yebba, Hurt Me So Good by Jazmine Sullivan, and Brokenhearted by Brandy. Music was so soothing to the piece of my heart that remained in my chest. It was the only place where I felt free. I had to realize that these feelings were valid and deserved to be acknowledged. It was okay to not be okay. Do I still have time?

Rinse stage

In the rinse stage, I wanted to cleanse myself of the negative thoughts and beliefs that had accumulated over the years. All of the pain and agony that I had experienced needed to drown in the deepest part of the sea. I knew that this would involve a lot of introspection and self-discovery. There were so many questions that I dug to a great depth to find answers to. Two very important questions were why I felt the need to give so much of myself to others and why I had such a hard time receiving in return. I had a hard time receiving because if anyone would ask if I needed anything, I would tell them no, or I'm fine.

Deep down, I did need them, but I was so used to giving that I had forgotten how to voice that need. So, I would just shut down when the opportunity presented itself. This last piece of my pure heart couldn't seem to find a reason to receive from others. Why was this so hard to accept? Cleanses are supposed to extract all of the toxins from within and any unhealthy characteristics, but somehow this dirty piece of clothing was still visible. Time was slipping.

Final spin

In the final spin stage, I started to put into practice all the things I had learned. I began to set boundaries with the people in my life, ensuring that my needs were also being met. I started to surround myself with those who valued me for who I was, not just for what I could give. I also engaged in activities that brought me joy and fulfillment outside of my relationships. I rediscovered hobbies that I had neglected and found new interests that excited me. This helped me build a stronger sense of self-worth and identity. While all of this was a favorable shift, negativity still wanted to overtake me, so I let it. I had instilled in my mind that there could never be a new me. The loud, prolonged beep went off from the washer. The cycles were complete, but the clock was still broken. Time ran out.

I began to understand the roots of my behavior and how they were tied to my past experiences and upbringing. This awareness was crucial in helping me break free from the cycle of giving until I was empty. I realized that I deserved to be taken care of, too, and that it was okay to ask for help and support. I also began to practice self-compassion. I stopped blaming myself for the failures in my relationships and started to forgive myself for my mistakes. This was a slow process, but with each small step, I felt a bit lighter. I learned that healing isn't a straight line.

It's a messy, convoluted process that often involves going back and forth between stages. Sometimes, it felt like I was making progress, only to be pulled back into the depths of despair. Other times, I felt motionless, as if no amount of effort could push me forward. This cycle occurred over and over again. The fumes that I was running on made me so restless to the point where I just knew that sleep no longer existed. I needed God to step in. I needed him to take this pain away. I needed him. God grant me the time.

Chapter 5

GOD

GOD,

I feel that I put too many expectations on people. I always get let down when I'm always there for someone, then when I need them the most and am crying silently, they're not there. I want people to convey the energy that I give. Everyone who has come into my life, I cherished them and gave them my all, but all that giving got me nothing in return. I always feel left behind while everyone and everything ahead of me prosper. I just want to win and be treated like the air that people breathe. I mean, air is important, right? Without it, there would be no us. I am more than enough for anyone, and I pray that person is preparing right now for me. I pray that they're praying for me and that they will never leave me behind. Praying that they will always be my footsteps while they carry me and that they never want to leave me alone. I guess the person that I'm praying for is YOU.

I've spent so much time investing in others, pouring my heart and soul into relationships, hoping for the same level of commitment and care in return. I have been through the worst of times and lived in thoughts of my father serenading the crowd at my invite-only funeral. The crowd who were always telling me to fight. The crowd that would pop up at my house unannounced and drag me out of bed. The crowd that always yearned for me to see the good in me. This is the crowd that never gave up on me, and even in the face of death, they were still there. The reality, though, was often disappointment and heartache. I couldn't let them in to give me that hope and time that I was searching for. It's a heavy burden to carry, feeling as if my worth is overlooked, my efforts unnoticed. But all along, the crowd was right there.

Perhaps this yearning for reciprocation isn't misplaced; maybe it's a call to deepen my connection with You. You, who always listen, who never turn away. You, who had my back when it was struck by the hand of a hurt, unreliable human being. Hurt people, hurt people, right? In my moments of silent tears and unspoken needs, You were always there, even when others were not. God, you loved me at my worst.

Love

I'm beginning to understand that the love and stability I was seeking from others can ultimately be found in You. The unwavering support, the understanding, the presence that I crave, You embody all of these. And while human relationships may falter, your love remains steadfast. Love is a very powerful word. I don't believe that people can choose who they want to love because they can end up choosing the wrong one. Love should come so naturally that the person you're able to share it with should be drawn to you.

It should feel so real that when you're away from them, you realize that missing them can never be an option. It's not just about presence; it's about a connection so deep that even in their absence, they are with you. Their essence lingers in every breath you take and in every thought you have. The bond transcends physical presence, embedding itself into the very fabric of your being. True love isn't about dependency or neediness; it's about a mutual understanding and respect that defies distance. It's the comfort of knowing that no matter where life takes you, a part of them is always with you, and a part of you is always with them. This kind of love doesn't fade with separation; it grows stronger, reinforcing the ties that bind your souls together.

When love feels this real, missing them becomes a mere illusion. Instead, you find solace in the quiet moments, knowing that your hearts beat in sync, no matter the miles between you. This is the love that we should all yearn for. The love that makes us whole, that makes us better, that makes every day brighter than the day before. God, the love you've shown is like no other, and I appreciate it more and more every day.

"I'll love you until there aren't any more sunsets, and the world is continuously night." -Je'Nae Brown

Chapter 6

Grace

Nicole sat on the edge of her bed, the weight of the past years pressing heavily on her shoulders. She had always believed that enduring the pain others inflicted upon her was her fault. Her reflection in the mirror showed tired eyes and a weary soul. One crisp autumn morning, as she walked through the park, a stranger approached her with a warm smile. “You dropped this,” he said, handing her a small, worn-out journal she didn’t even realize she had lost. “Thank you,” she murmured, surprised by the kindness in his eyes. It was a simple act, yet it felt like a lifeline thrown into her sea of despair.

As Nicole flipped through the pages of her journal later that evening, she stumbled upon a passage about grace. She had written it long ago but had forgotten its significance. Can grace renew my darkest night? That question echoed in her mind. Could it be that grace was what she needed all along? In the weeks that followed, Nicole embarked on a journey of self-discovery. She sought out stories of grace, prayed fervently, and spoke with those who had found peace through acceptance.

Slowly, she began to let go of her guilt and embrace the notion that she was worthy of love and forgiveness. One evening, Nicole stood by the old oak tree in the town's park, the setting sun casting a golden glow around her. She felt a newfound sense of peace and purpose. Grace had found her in her darkest moments, and she was now ready to share that grace with others.

At times, I've felt so unworthy, unloved, and guilty. But it wasn't because of what I did to others, it was because of the trials, hurt, and pain that they put me through. It was all my fault for enduring so much for so long, and I wasn't innocent. Grace is an unmerited favor, and most of the time it can be difficult to understand. God gives us grace in the most crucial times.

No matter how many instances we've gotten off course, if we accept his grace, it could lead us back onto our correct path. Acceptance can unfold an undeniable love for ourselves and others. We have to accept the things that we cannot see, so that grace can overcome guilt. Always be open and available to receive grace. You can't wait until life isn't hard anymore before you decide to be happy.

Life is going to hit you with every obstacle possible. Some obstacles are big and some are small, but they're still obstacles.

You can't pick and choose which one you're going to endure because when they hit, they hit. What you can choose to do is fight and push through. When you show something or someone that you're not going to lose without a fight, sometimes they will back down. They'll say, I'm not messing with them, they're crazy. Even if they don't back down, they'll know that they've got to bring their all, and what their opponent sees in front of them is grace.

There were times when I was so scared to face my adversaries that I just let them win. I had convinced myself that if I gave up, they would just get their victory and leave. I was so wrong because once they got their victory, they had concluded me to be weak and stayed as if it was a high for them. I believe that you can't see something in someone else unless it exists in you. What I saw in them was a strong individual who had the determination to win at all costs.

What they saw in me was a weak individual who didn't have any self-worth, just doubt. I often felt that the fight wasn't mine to win and that it was their time to shine. Those individuals shone so much that every time I looked up, there was a cloud of darkness surrounding me. There was no light. So, I couldn't see my way through, and with every opponent that I came across, their light got brighter and brighter. This darkness covered my grace.

I mentioned before that I always wanted to make the next person feel better. I always wanted them to see their light and for them to know that I always had their back. While doing this for others, the back that needed this same reassurance, the pain from others made it weak. You could tell my weakness from the way I walked. My posture was always irregular. I could not find the fight in me, and I felt that if I tried, I would end up taking their shine. My heart couldn't steal their shine, so losing was destined. It was my determination and duty to lose. It was like going up against Mayweather, knowing that I was going to lose, but the difference with that was that Mayweather's opponent was still going to get paid either way. In my situation, there was no payout for the transfer of my weakness. I was embarrassing my grace.

I remember one of my opponents asking me what I liked about them. I answered them and said, "You have this light that shines over you, and that's what draws me to you." I believe that the confusion with my darkness versus their light was that I couldn't overcome my adversaries because I had instilled all of my energy and light into them. I was always the one saying, "Good morning, I hope you have a prosperous and amazing day, or make today a better day than before." My affirmations were always on point, but I never received one affirmation from my opponents. I was the one who pushed and uplifted them so that they could become their best selves.

I went above and beyond for my opponents with a smile on my face and never thought twice about what I had done. They never poured into me, like I poured into them. Therefore, they were sucking me dry and dimming my light until all I saw was darkness. This is where my weakness came from. I had no more energy left to give, and I was steadily chasing their light because my darkness prevented me from seeing mine. My grace no longer wanted to be a part of this.

Marvin Sapp has a song called Place of Worship. In the song, he tells us to *"Look into your pain and find your praise, Every low place in your life prepared you for your high place, Every tear you cried was water for the garden of your victory, And even though you're in the valley, Victory comes through your adversity, Go find your place of worship."* I would often listen to the song, but never really knew the meaning behind the words. The album is called "Thirsty," and I played it every day. One particular day, I knew that I had to find my grace. This was the day that my light needed to shine brighter than any of my opponents, so I started to read the words of the song.

The words were so beautiful and encouraging that I began to break them down to understand them more. I had to look into my pain, worry, sorrow, and defeat to find the person who was screaming for attention. The person who had fallen from grace. The person who could no longer see her light because she was passing it on to her unworthy opponents. All of these losses were preparing me for my win. They were getting me ready for my self-worth. All of the tears I cried were just watering my big reveal, and even though I was in the darkness, my victory was right in front of me. I was just the one who had to see it and believe it. I had to fight back to find my grace.

I was so exhausted from the unworthiness and pain; I thought I couldn't win my fight. I feel that it's so powerful to acknowledge that grace can bring healing and lead us back to a path of love and acceptance. How can you love and accept yourself when you keep looking for yourself in your opponent? You might think that your opponent cares, but they're your opponent for a reason. I had to push through and fight to rediscover my light, and I did.

Throughout my rediscovery of my light, I cried oceans, not tears. It was at that moment that I knew God had favored me. It felt as if my old skin was shedding and revealing the me I had misplaced. But it wasn't the old me; it was the reinvented me, a new version of myself. I remember walking up to the mirror, in awe of my reflection, and saying I missed you.

This made me listen to "Place of Worship" even more, and the more I listened to that song, the more I revealed myself to myself. I wasn't scared to face my adversary and fight for my light to shine through their darkness. I mentioned before that you can't see something in someone else unless it exists in you. So, the strength that I saw in them, their light I had praised them for, and their self-worth that I had yearned for, was in me all along. What I had seen in them was what I had to reveal within me.

The weakness that they had instilled in me was overpowering my grace, but it was indeed their weakness. Their weak souls needed my light to win. They needed my strength to survive. I no longer wanted to be their shadow, yearning for their light. I started to fight back because I never knew how powerful my strength was. I became Mayweather and not the opponent. There was suddenly an openness to receive and transform my power into a cup full of grace.

Chapter 7

A Cup Full

Every time I order a drink from any drive-thru, I anticipate the cup to be full. Whether it's full from the ice or the liquid, I want it to be to the rim. When I receive a drink that isn't full, I politely ask them to fill it up. It's so easy to ask for the cup to be full when it's not to my acceptance. "Fill it up!" That's what I want to scream to whoever is handling the cup. If only my method of cup filling were this easy when it comes to my life.

I can barely fill my cup up to the halfway point. When I yell, "Fill it up!" to myself, I don't even budge. Why can't I fill up my cup? It works in the drive-thru. I mean, the cup is mine because I paid for it, but when it comes to mentally filling my cup up so that I can be whole, I freeze. Maybe I can't move because I'm waiting for someone else to fill it up for me. But I feel that is where the issue lies. I should never wait for someone else to fill my cup. If I allow them to fill it up to make me whole, then they have the power to pour some out when they're not satisfied. I don't want anyone to be in charge of my cup, and if I can't fill it myself, then I just won't fill it at all. I have to yell, "Fill it up!" to myself every day until my cup is full and continuously yell until it's overflowing to my acceptance.

True fulfillment and peace come from within, and while others can certainly add to your life, they can't fully satisfy you if you're not already nurturing yourself. Imagine your heart or spirit as a cup. While others can pour into you, offering love, support, and encouragement. It's important to recognize that their contributions can never fill you. People may try to help, but the real work of being fulfilled starts with how you care for and nurture yourself. Self-love, self-awareness, and personal growth are what truly fill you up. No one else can pour into you enough to make you whole, because the deepest fulfillment comes from the relationship you have with yourself.

Moreover, this process is not just about personal effort; it's about being open to God's presence and guidance. God, as a source of infinite love and strength, can fill you in ways that are beyond human capacity. As you connect with God and align with his purpose, you start to experience the process of being filled, not from external sources, but from a deeper spiritual well. In this way, you're not just waiting for others to pour into you; you're actively participating in your healing and growth, receiving from both God and you. When you are filled in this way, you are then able to give and receive in healthier, more balanced ways, because you're no longer relying on others to meet your deepest needs. Instead, you can offer from a place of abundance and wholeness.

In most of my moments of desperation, I turned to prayer. I asked God for help, guidance, and strength. I didn't expect a miracle, but I felt a quiet peace wash over me as I spoke to him. It was in that silence that I realized the most important part of filling my cup wasn't about waiting for others to do it for me; it was about embracing God's love and allowing his presence to fill the spaces within me that nothing else could. I was no longer searching for validation in external sources because I knew God had already given me everything I needed to be whole. There's a scripture that has always stuck with me: **Philippians 4:13 KJV**, ***"I can do all things through Christ who strengthens me"***. I used to make my boys recite this before they got out of the car, as I was dropping them off at school. I wanted to reassure myself and them that anytime we were faced with self-doubt or uncertainty. God's love and strength were constantly available to us. I wanted us to know that we couldn't do anything alone and that we needed him to hold our hands every step of the way. For with God, all things are possible.

I wanted to capture the challenge of self-fulfillment and the importance of taking personal responsibility for our well-being. It's a poignant reminder that while it's easy to demand what we want from others, it's often more difficult to demand it from ourselves. The metaphor of the cup emphasizes the need for self-care and the empowerment that comes from taking control of our own lives. While I didn't have much to elaborate on filling my cup, I did write a poem just for entertainment.

If you've made it this far, then it's either something I wrote that you agreed with, or perhaps it was just an enjoyable read. Whatever you've gained from this, I hope it inspires reflection and growth. I also want to gently remind you that if there's anything you disagree with, that's perfectly fine. You're entitled to your perspective. We all have our journeys, and differing viewpoints can sometimes offer valuable insights. If you ever feel challenged or triggered by someone's strength or confidence, I encourage you to reflect on what that emotion is teaching you. You have the power to transform envy or resentment into inspiration, using it as fuel for your growth and self-assurance. Embrace your journey, and if you find admiration in others, let it remind you of the greatness that lies within you as well. Keep being true to yourself and focused on becoming the best version of who you are.

Fill My Cup

A cup full, that's what I seek,

In the drive-thru, every week.

Ice or liquid to the brim,

A simple wish, not too dim.

I ask politely, "Fill it up."

They oblige, no need to sup.

Yet in my life, I find it tough,

To fill my cup, it's never enough.

I scream inside, "Fill it up!"

But my heart, it won't erupt.

Why can't I pour for me,

What I demand so easily?

Waiting for others to fill the space,

Leaves me longing, out of place.

If they fill, they hold the key,

To take away what's dear to me.

No longer will I wait and see,

I'll take the charge, I'll fill for me.

Each day, a drop, a mindful act,

Until my cup is full, intact.

"Fill it up!" I'll shout and say,

To myself, come what may.

Until it overflows with grace,

And in the mirror, I find my place.

A cup full, not just in hand,

But in my heart, where I stand.

Filled with love, with strength anew,

A cup full, because I grew.

My Prayer

GOD, help me remember that I am enough, not because of the validation I receive from others, but because I am valued by You. Guide me to find strength in this knowledge and to continue loving and giving without expecting anything in return, knowing that You are my constant. In this journey, I pray for the wisdom to set healthy boundaries and the courage to seek connections that uplift and nurture me. I pray for the discernment to recognize those who truly value me and the strength to let go of those who do not. And most importantly, I pray for the grace to forgive. Forgive myself for the times I overextended. Forgive others for the times they've let me down. Forgive the weakness that overcomes my strength. And forgive the inability to see the things that I cannot change. In doing so, I hope to create space for healing, growth, and the possibility of relationships that reflect the mutual love and respect I desire. Thank you for being my guiding light, my source of hope, and my unwavering support. For with You, I know I am never alone, and I am always enough. GOD always removes the nothing, gives me hope, and whenever I start, let me make it to the finish line completely trusting in You.

Amen.

www.ingramcontent.com/pod-product-compliance
Lightning Source LLC
LaVergne TN
LVHW010944110826
845149LV00013B/2745

* 9 7 9 8 9 8 9 8 7 1 4 2 1 *